IS-907 –
Active Shooter:
What You Can Do

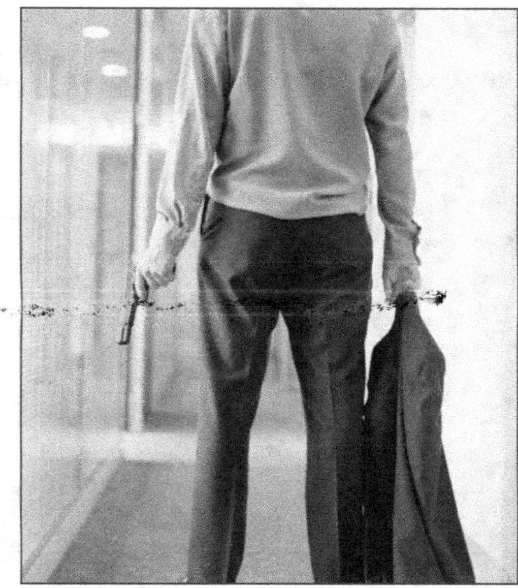

DISPATCHER:
"911, what is the nature of your emergency?"

CALLER:
"There's somebody with a gun in the main entrance to the mall and I don't . . ."

Active shooter situations are unpredictable and evolve quickly.

Are you prepared?

Course Objectives

- **Describe actions to take when confronted with:**
  - **An active shooter.**
  - **Law enforcement officers who are responding to the situation.**
- **Recognize potential workplace violence indicators.**
- **Describe actions to take to prevent and prepare for potential active shooter incidents.**
- **Describe how to manage the consequences of an active shooter incident.**

Active Shooter Incidents

Where we:

- **Shop**
- **Exercise free speech**
- **Learn**
- **Work**

About Active Shooter Incidents

- More frequent.
- Anger, revenge, ideology, untreated mental illness.

Employees can help prevent and prepare.

Active Shooter Situations

- **Unpredictable.**
- **Evolve quickly.**
- **Continue until stopped by law enforcement, suicide, or intervention.**

Active Shooter Booklet

Guidance for:

- **Individuals**
- **Managers**
- **Employees**

Course Topics

Discussion: Response

FEMA

How To Respond

- **Evacuate**
- **Hide Out**
- **Take Action**

Evacuate (1 of 2)

- Have an escape route and plan in mind.

- Leave your belongings behind.

- Help others escape, if possible.

- Evacuate regardless of others.

- Warn/prevent individuals from entering.

Evacuate (2 of 2)

- Do not attempt to move wounded people.
- Keep your hands visible.
- Follow police instructions.
- Call 911 when safe.

Hide Out

Your hiding spot should:

- **Be out of the active shooter's view.**

- **Provide protection if shots are fired.**

- **Not restrict options for movement.**

Keeping Yourself Safe While Hiding

If the shooter is nearby:

- Lock the door.
- Hide behind large item (e.g., cabinet, desk).
- Silence cell phone/pager.
- Remain quiet.

Important Information

Provide law enforcement or 911 operators with:

- Location of shooter.
- Number of shooters.
- Physical description of shooters.
- Number and types of weapons.
- Number of potential victims.

Take Action

As an absolute last resort:

- **Act as aggressively as possible.**
- **Improvise weapons and throw items.**
- **Yell.**
- **Commit to your actions.**

Discussion: Reaction of Managers

Discussion: When Law Enforcement Arrives

Law Enforcement's Role

Immediate purpose:

- **Stop the active shooter.**
- **Proceed to area where last shots heard.**
- **First priority is to eliminate the threat.**

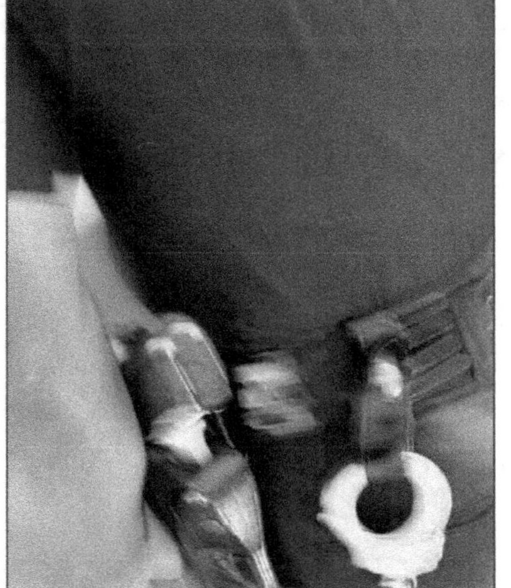

Additional Officers and Rescue Teams

Teams may:

- Wear bulletproof vests, helmets, and other equipment.
- Be armed with rifles, shotguns, and/or handguns.
- Use pepper spray.
- Shout commands.
- Push individuals to the ground for their safety.

Reacting to Law Enforcement

- Remain calm.
- Put down any items.
- Raise hands and spread fingers.
- Avoid quick movements.
- Avoid pointing, screaming, or yelling.
- Proceed in direction from which officers are entering.

Safe Location

Area controlled by law enforcement until:

- **The situation is under control.**
- **All witnesses are identified and questioned.**

Course Topics

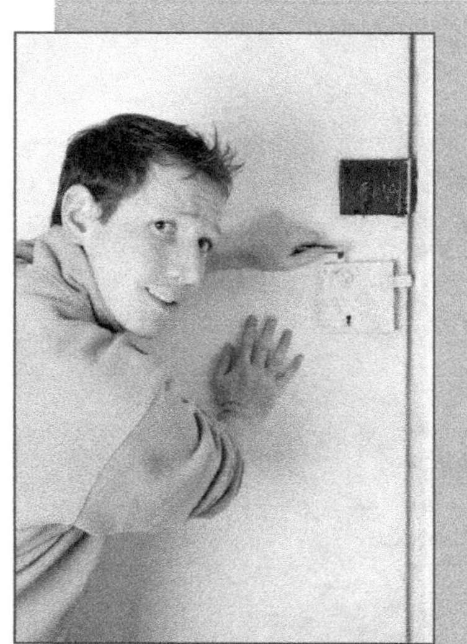

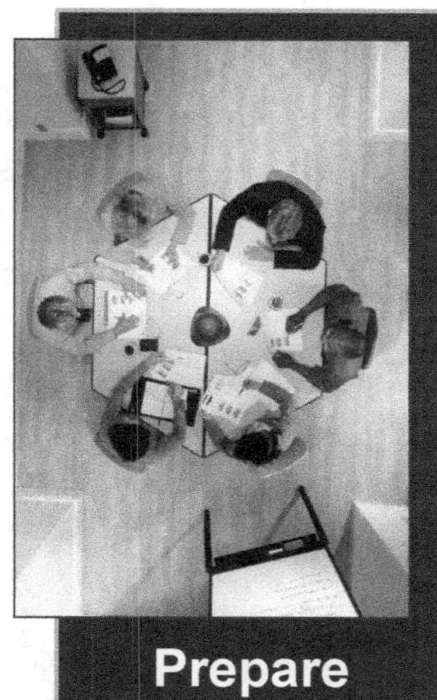

Discussion: Preparation

How To Prepare

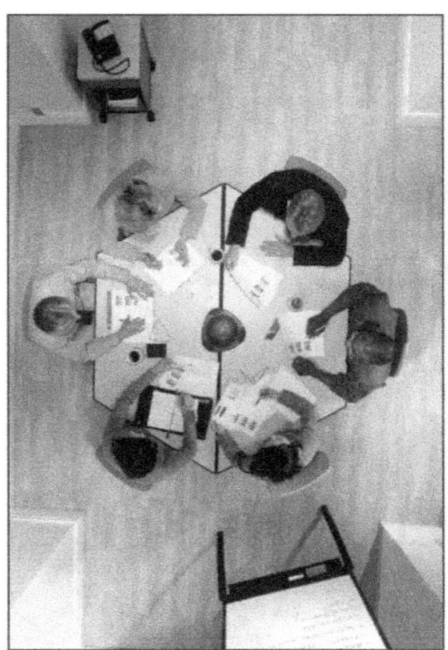

- **Develop an Emergency Action Plan.**
- **Conduct training.**
- **Recognize indicators of potential workplace violence.**

Developing an Emergency Action Plan

Get input from:

- **Human resources department.**
- **Training department.**
- **Facility owners/operators.**
- **Property manager.**
- **Local law enforcement and emergency responders.**

Components of an Effective Plan

- A preferred method for reporting different types of emergencies

- An evacuation policy and procedure

- Emergency escape procedures and route assignments

- Contact information for individuals to be contacted under the Emergency Action Plan

- Information concerning local area hospitals

- An emergency notification system to alert various parties of an emergency

Conducting Training

Employee training should include:

- **Identifying the sound of gunfire.**
- **Reacting quickly.**
- **Calling 911.**
- **Reacting when law enforcement arrives.**
- **Adopting a survival mindset during a crisis.**

Meet Everyone's Needs

Ensure that plans assess and provide for functional needs:

- Hearing or sight
- Mobility
- Limited or no English proficiency

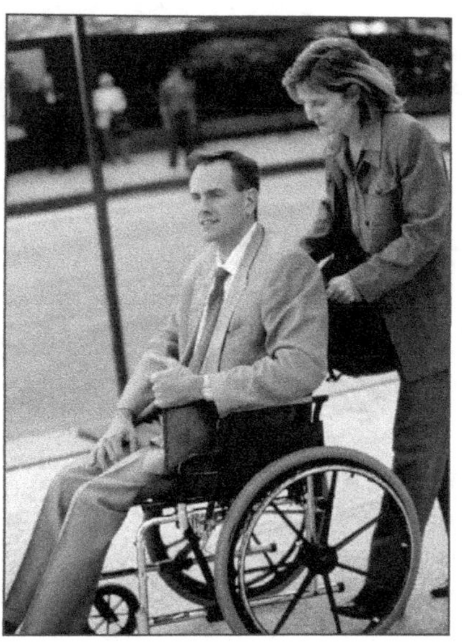

Facility Manager Responsibilities (1 of 2)

- Institute access controls.
- Distribute critical items.
- Assemble crisis kits.
- Activate the emergency notification system.
- Ensure two evacuation routes.
- Coordinate with the facility's security department.

Facility Manager Responsibilities (2 of 2)

- Post evacuation routes.
- Place removable floor plans near entrances and exits.
- Include law enforcement and first responders in training.
- Encourage active shooter training.
- Foster a respectful workplace.
- Be aware of workplace violence indicators.

Recognizing Indicators of Violence

Workplace Violence Indicators

- May be current or former employee.

- May display characteristics of potentially violent behavior.

Human Resources Responsibilities

- Conduct effective background checks.
- Create system for reporting violent behavior.
- Make counseling available.
- Develop plan dealing with an active shooter situation.

Activity: Indicators of Workplace Violence

<u>Instructions:</u> Working as a team:

1. Create a list of 10 indicators of potentially violent behavior.

2. Record the list on chart paper.

3. Select a spokesperson and be prepared to present your list in 5 minutes.

Activity: Self-Assessment

<u>Instructions</u>: **Working individually:**

1. **Take 5 minutes to complete the self-assessment in your Student Manual.**

2. **Jot down action steps you can take for areas needing improvement.**

3. **Remember, this is a self-assessment, so be honest!**

Course Topics

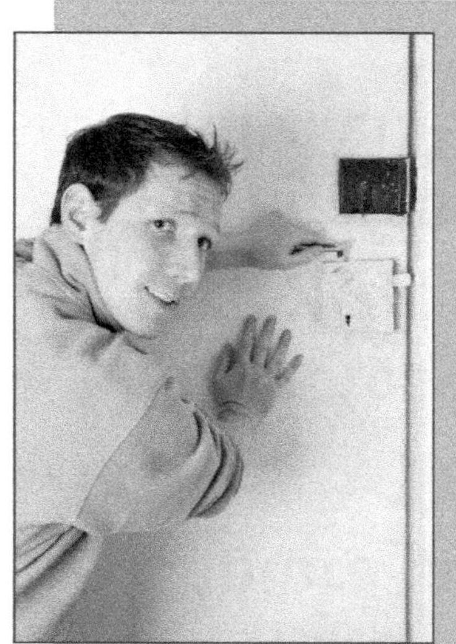

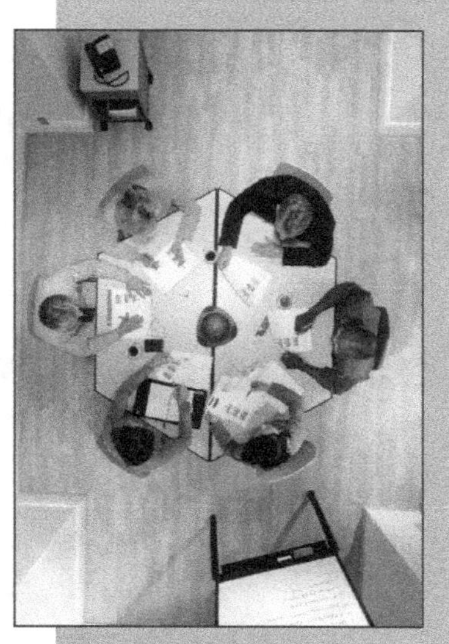

How To Follow Up

Important to:

- **Manage consequences**
- **Capture lessons learned**

Results:

- **Promotes well-being of those involved**
- **Facilitates preparedness for future emergencies**

Managing the Consequences

- Determine who is missing or injured.

- Determine a method for notifying families.

- Assess psychological state of individuals.

- Identify and fill critical personnel or operational gaps.

Lessons Learned

- **Document response activities.**
- **Identify successes and failures.**
- **Provide analysis of existing plan effectiveness.**
- **Describe plans for improvements.**

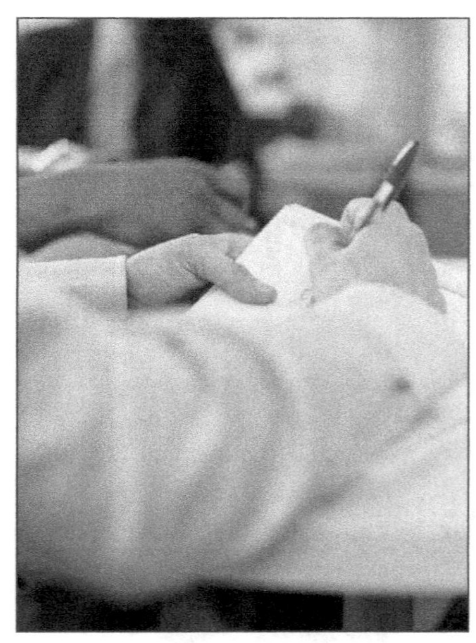

Workplace Violence Resources

Resources include:

- **Active Shooter Booklet**
- **Active Shooter Pocket Guide**
- **Active Shooter Poster**

Course Summary

- Evacuate, hide, take action.
- Call 911 when it is safe to do so!
- Always take note of the two nearest exits.
- Be aware of your environment and possible dangers.